TIMELINES

World War I

Stewart Ross

ARCTURUS

This edition first published by Arcturus Publishing
Distributed by Black Rabbit Books
123 South Broad Street
Mankato
Minnesota MN 56001

Printed in China

Library of Congress Cataloging-in-Publication Data

Ross, Stewart.
  World War I / by Stewart Ross.
     p. cm. -- (Timelines)
Includes bibliographical references and index.
ISBN 978-1-84193-729-8 (alk. paper)
1. World War, 1914-1918--Juvenile literature. 2. World War, 1914-1918--
Chronology--Juvenile literature. I. Title. II. Title: World War one. III. Title: World
War 1. IV. Series.

D522.7.R68 2007
940.3--dc22

                    2007007555

9 8 7 6 5 4 3 2

Series concept: Alex Woolf
Project manager and editor: Liz Miles
Designer: Simon Borrough
Picture researcher: Liz Miles
Consultant: James Vaughan
Cartographer: LMS

Picture credits:
Corbis: cover (Bettmann/Corbis), 4 (Hulton-Deutsch Collection/Corbis),
5 (Corbis), 6, 7 (Hulton-Deutsch Collection/Corbis), 9 (Corbis), 10, 11
(Bettmann/Corbis), 12, 13 (Hulton-Deutsch Collection/Corbis), 14
(Bettmann/Corbis), 15 (Corbis), 16 (Bettmann/Corbis), 17 (Underwood &
Underwood/Corbis), 18 (Bettmann/Corbis), 19 (Corbis), 20 (Hulton-Deutsch
Collection), 22 (Bettmann/Corbis), 23, 24 (Corbis), 25 (Bettmann/Corbis), 27
(Hulton-Deutsch Collection/Corbis), 30 (Corbis), 31, 32, 34 (Hulton-Deutsch
Collection/Corbis), 35 (Corbis), 36 (Hulton-Deutsch Collection/Corbis), 37,
38, 39 (Bettmann/Corbis), 40 (Hulton-Deutsch Collection/Corbis), 41 (Corbis),
42 (Bettmann/Corbis), 43 (Hulton-Deutsch Collection/Corbis), 44 (Corbis), 45
(Bettmann/Corbis).
TopFoto: 21 (Topham Picturepoint), 26 (RIA Novosti), 28, 29 (Topham
Picturepoint), 33 (HIP).

Contents

Franco-Prussian War Begins

The roots of World War I go back to the nineteenth century. At their heart was fierce rivalry between the great powers of Europe. This rivalry came to a head on July 19, 1870, when the French emperor Napoleon III declared war on Prussia, the most powerful state in Germany. He believed the southern German states, such as Bavaria and Baden, would take his side. He was mistaken. The French armies were slow to mobilize and the well-organized Prussians swept into eastern France and won two decisive victories at Metz and Sedan. Napoleon III was captured and his government collapsed. France became a republic for the third time.

THE GERMAN EMPIRE

Although the Third Republic fought on into the following year, its efforts were in vain. By the Treaty of Frankfurt, May 10, 1871, France surrendered Alsace and Lorraine and agreed to pay the victors large reparations. Meanwhile, an even more important event had taken place. On January 18, at the palace of Versailles, in France, the triumphant and united German states accepted Prussia's King William I as emperor of a German empire. The new Germany was undisputedly the major power in continental Europe.

Scare tactics

"If you rub it in both at home and abroad that you intend to be 'first in' and hit your enemy in the belly and kick him when he's down and boil your prisoners in oil (*if you take any*) and torture his women and children, then people will steer clear of you."

British First Sea Lord, Admiral Jackie Fisher, in an exaggerated explanation of how peace can be preserved by building up military might.
Quoted in A. Marder, ed., *Fear God and Dread Nought: The Correspondence of Admiral of the Fleet Lord Fisher of Kilverstone*, 3 vols (London, 1951–1959).

Heavy cannons used during the siege of Paris at the end of the Franco-Prussian War.

SHIFT IN WORLD POWER

For centuries, France had dominated the continent. Now, with the emergence of the German Empire under the guiding hand of the Prussian chancellor, Otto von Bismarck, this had changed. In terms of military power, population, and economic strength, Germany had replaced France.

To thwart French hopes of revenge, Bismarck kept the French isolated by a series of agreements with Russia, Austria-Hungary, and Italy. However, in 1890, Bismarck fell out with Germany's new emperor, William II, and resigned. With the mastermind of German unification gone, France began building up alliances of its own. First came a military agreement with Russia (1894); then, more significant, an *entente* (understanding, 1904) with Britain, the major world power. When Britain and Russia reached an agreement three years later, Europe was divided into two hostile camps: the Triple Alliance and the Triple Entente. Economic and imperial rivalry fueled the tension. As each side built up its armaments, the chances of a major conflict rose.

CROSS-REFERENCE
THE TRIPLE ALLIANCE AND THE TRIPLE ENTENTE: PAGES 6–7

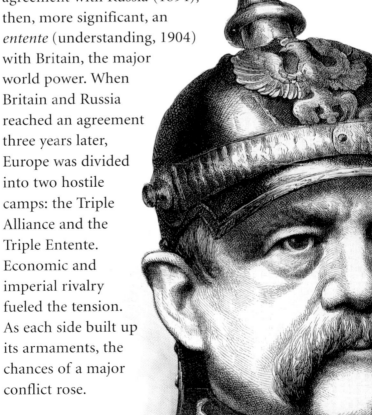

The Iron Chancellor, Otto von Bismarck, who masterminded the unification of Germany into a single empire.

Assassination of Archduke Ferdinand

28 JUNE 1914

Archduke Franz Ferdinand was heir to the throne of Austria-Hungary, Germany's closest ally. In June 1914, he paid a state visit to Bosnia, a state recently annexed by Austria-Hungary. While visiting the capital, Sarajevo, he and his wife were shot dead by Gavrilo Princip, a Bosnian nationalist. Princip's gang had links with Serbia, Bosnia's powerful neighbor and Russia's ally.

POWDER KEG OF EUROPE

Bosnia, Herzegovina, and Serbia were in the Balkans, a mountainous area of eastern Europe once part of the Turkish Empire. As this empire declined, the Balkan peoples struggled for independence while Russia and Austria-Hungary competed for control of the region. This instability made the Balkans the "powder keg" of Europe—the region most likely to blow up, causing further explosions elsewhere.

The Balkan situation was particularly dangerous because of Russia and Austria-Hungary's alliances. Russia had agreements with France and Britain (the Triple Entente) and Austria-Hungary was part of the Triple Alliance with Germany and Italy. Tension between these armed camps—the Triple Alliance and the Triple Entente—had already come close to crisis.

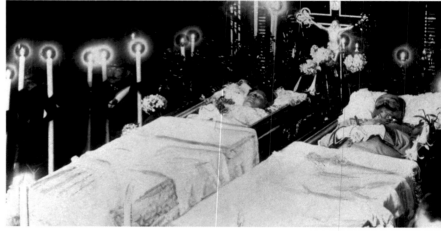

Tensions rose in 1905–1906 and 1911 when France and Britain had forced Germany to back down over colonial disputes in North Africa. Russia had also backed down when Austria-Hungary had annexed Bosnia and

The deaths that changed the world: the bodies of Austria's Archduke Franz Ferdinand and his wife Sophie after their assassination.

Accept or die

"The Royal Serbian Government will . . . pledge itself:
1. to **suppress every publication** which shall incite to hatred . . . of the [Austro-Hungarian] Monarchy. . . .
4. to remove from the military and administrative service . . . all . . . officials who have been . . . carrying on the propaganda against Austria-Hungary, whose names the [Austro-Hungarian] . . . Government reserves the right to make known."

Part of Austria-Hungary's ultimatum to Serbia, which it had to accept, or face bloody conquest.
Quoted in www.lib.byu.edu/~rdh/wwi/1914/austro-hungarian-ultimatum.html

Herzegovina in 1908. More recently, two Balkan Wars (1912 and 1913) had left Serbia—Russia's ally—stronger than ever, threatening Austria-Hungary's power in the region.

CHAIN REACTION

Franz Ferdinand's assassination sparked off a chain reaction that led to a Europe-wide war. With guaranteed support from Germany, Austria-Hungary sent Serbia an impossible ultimatum. When Serbia rejected it, Austria-Hungary declared war. On July 30, Russia began to mobilize to help Serbia. Germany threatened war unless Russia demobilized, then declared war on August 1. France mobilized in support of Russia, so Germany declared war on France. The German armies struck at France through Belgium, whose neutrality Britain had guaranteed. At midnight on August 4, Britain too found itself at war with Germany.

At this stage, Italy and the U.S. refused to be drawn into the conflict. Because of Europe's worldwide empires, however, the shock of war soon spread right around the planet.

CROSS-REFERENCE GERMAN INVASION OF BELGIUM: PAGES 10–11

Death or glory! Infantrymen of the Austro-Hungarian Army on parade before being transported to the Russian Front.

Battle of Tannenberg Begins

Before the war, the Russian forces were seen as a steamroller: slow to move but unstoppable once they did. The reality proved very different. First, the Russians moved quicker than expected, advancing into East Prussia and forcing the Germans back. Second, after this minor success, Russian progress came to a juddering halt at the Battles of Tannenberg and the Masurian Lakes.

HINDENBURG'S ATTACK

On August 26, 1914, the new commander of the German Eighth Army, General von Hindenburg, launched a massive attack on General Samsonov's Russian Second Army. Hindenburg had two big advantages. His wireless operators were intercepting the enemy's messages, and he knew that Samsonov and Rennenkampf, the commander of another Russian army nearby, disliked each other. Rennenkampf was unlikely to come to the rescue if things went wrong for Samsonov.

Things did go wrong for Samsonov. After some success, his army was entirely surrounded and forced to surrender, losing 125,000 men and 500 guns. Samsonov shot himself. A few

The major fronts and battlefields of World War I. The borders are those that existed in 1914.

weeks later, Hindenburg turned on Rennenkampf and defeated him at the Battle of the Masurian Lakes. The Russians retreated from German soil, which remained free from the enemy for the rest of the war.

THE EASTERN FRONT

The battle lines between Russia, Germany, and Austria-Hungary were known as the Eastern Front. On its southern sector, below Tannenberg, the Russians met with greater success. By the end of 1914, they had advanced into the Austrian province of Galicia, almost reaching the Carpathian Mountains. In May the following year, after the snows had melted, the Germans and Austro-Hungarians struck back.

The assault was called the Gorlice-Tarnów Offensive. Planned by General von Falkenhayn and led by General von Mackensen, it was a spectacular success. By mid-September, the Russians had been driven from Galicia and Poland at a cost of 1 million men killed and another million captured. The Austro-Hungarians had success in the Balkans, too. After failing to conquer Serbia in 1914, they tried again in 1915, helped by Germany and Bulgaria. By the end of the year, Serbian resistance had been broken and the country was in enemy hands.

CROSS-REFERENCE GENERAL VON HINDENBURG: PAGE 26

Attack old-style: a German infantry charge at the Battle of the Marne. Machine-gun fire would soon make such tactics unrealistic.

Battle of the Marne Begins

The Battle of the Marne, from September 5–9, 1914, was one of the major turning points of the war. It began when the German First Army abandoned its plan of sweeping round Paris. Instead, General Kluck decided to move to the east of the French capital. This left him open to attack from the French forces to his right.

Kluck fell back to deal with the threat, leaving a gap between himself and the German Second Army to his left. Enemy planes—in one of the first important uses of aircraft in wartime—spotted this gap and the Anglo-French Allies advanced into it. After four days of fighting around the Marne River, the Germans were forced to withdraw. Paris had been saved and the German advance finally halted.

WAR PLANS

The moment war broke out, the French and German high commands began executing their carefully prepared battle plans. The French had Plan XVII, a major assault to recapture Alsace and Lorraine. The Germans had the Schlieffen Plan, drawn up in 1905 but later altered by General von Moltke. It involved a large German force passing through neutral Belgium, surrounding Paris, and attacking the main French forces from the rear.

Neither plan worked. The French attack in the east was halted in the Battle of the Frontiers. The Schlieffen

Plan started to come unstuck when the Belgians put up stouter resistance than expected. After driving back the tiny British army (known as the British Expeditionary Force), the Germans tried to cut back to the east of Paris. This led to the Battle of the Marne and withdrawal. An Allied counterattack on the Aisne River was driven back with heavy losses.

TRENCH WARFARE

Commanders on both sides realized that they were fighting an entirely new type of warfare. The technology of defense—machine guns, mortars, heavy artillery, and barbed wire—made straightforward attack suicidal. The opposing armies took refuge in long lines of trenches that soon stretched right across France and Belgium. Much of the rest of the war on the Western Front was spent trying to break the murderous deadlock of trench warfare.

British soldiers take up defensive positions during the Battle of the Marne. Note the lack of steel helmets at this stage of the war.

THE GERMAN ADVANCE 1914

August 5, 1914 ▶ First land operation of the war begins as German troops enter Belgium and attack the forts around the city of Liège.

August 7, 1914 ▶ The first British troops arrive in France but not in large enough numbers to have a major impact on the conflict.

August 14, 1914 ▶ Battle of the Frontiers begins, resulting in a failure of the French offensive into Alsace and Lorraine.

August 26, 1914 ▶ In Britain's largest battle since Waterloo (1815), the British Expeditionary Force fight off an attack by the German First Army at Le Cateau.

September 5, 1914 ▶ Battle of the Marne begins, halting the German advance on the Marne River.

September 18, 1914 ▶ As Battle of the River Aisne ends, both sides realize conventional infantry attacks are likely to fail.

Early trench warfare: German soldiers in defensive positions on the Western Front, 1914.

CROSS-REFERENCE
TRENCH WARFARE:
PAGES 12–13,
28–29, 32–33

The balance of forces (in millions) at the outbreak of war, August 1914

Country	Population	Military manpower after mobilization
Triple Alliance and its allies		
Austria-Hungary	49.9	3.35
Germany	67	4.5
Italy	35	0.87
Turkey	21.3	0.3 (estimate)
Triple Entente and its allies		
Belgium	7.5	0.177
France	39.6	3.78
Russia	167	5
Serbia	5	0.46
UK	46.4	0.98*

* includes Indian Army and forces of Australia, New Zealand, and South Africa

First Battle of Ypres Begins

On October 12, as the two opposing armies on the Western Front moved quickly in the "Race to the Sea," the Germans made a final effort to outflank (get round) the Anglo-Belgian line at Armentières. They failed. Within a few days, the trenches of both the Allies (Triple Entente) and the Germans ran in unbroken, parallel lines from the Swiss border to the North Sea. However, the Allies' line was far from straight and the Germans quickly identified a weakness near the town of Ypres.

THE DEADLY SALIENT

The bulge in the line around Ypres, known as a "salient," was liable to attack from three sides. Beginning on October 20, the Germans first attacked the Belgian troops in the north of the salient and drove them back. Ten days later the attacks restarted and continued on and off to the end of November. The Allies were pushed back but no breakthrough was achieved. Hundreds of thousands of men on both sides were killed and wounded.

1915—STALEMATE

By the end of 1914, the German forces occupied a huge chunk of eastern France between the Champagne region, near Rheims, and the Belgian border, near Lille. It was on this sector that the French and British concentrated their attacks as they pushed toward Paris. The French commander, Marshal Joffre, launched an attack in the Champagne region five days before Christmas, 1914. It continued until mid-March, gaining

Belgian troops take up defensive positions beside a canal near Ypres in a successful bid to stop the German Army reaching the Channel ports.

Horror at Ypres

"I threw myself on the ground and started firing my rifle in the direction of the machine guns. Then I felt a strike on my right hand, blood runs hot down from it, the rifle falls. . . . **Around me some have become silent,** others cry and ask for help. . . . I feel another strike, this time in my thigh. Got again!"

From the diary of F. L. Cassel of German Infantry Regiment 143 who was twice wounded during an Allied counterattack at Ypres, November 1914. Quoted in Malcolm Brown, ed., *The Imperial War Museum Book of the First World War* (Sidgwick and Jackson, 1991).

DEADLOCK ON THE WESTERN FRONT 1914–1915

October 20, 1914 ▶ First Battle of Ypres begins as Germans attack the salient around the town.

December 20, 1914 ▶ First Battle of Champagne begins as Marshal Joffre launches his unsuccessful winter offensive.

March 10, 1915 ▶ Small British gains made on the first day of the Battle of Neuve-Chapelle.

May 9, 1915 ▶ First day of the First Battle of Artois sees quick gains for the French and British before stagnation.

May 22, 1915 ▶ Second Battle of Ypres begins as the Germans launch a surprise attack on the Ypres salient and make some advances.

September 21, 1915 ▶ Huge bombardment opens the Second Battle of Champagne in which the French advance almost 3 miles (5 km) in places.

September 25, 1915 ▶ Last offensive of the year launched in the Artois region has a similar fate.

little land and costing some 90,000 men. Meanwhile, the British had advanced 1.3 miles (2.1 km) after a surprise attack on the village of Neuve-Chapelle. The Germans responded with their own surprise attack on the Ypres salient. Helped by poison gas, a new secret weapon, small gains were made at a huge cost (59,000 British, 35,000 Germans). There were similar results in May when the French and British attacked in the Artois region. The assault was called off after the French had lost 100,000 men. Yet another attack in the same region in the autumn produced more horrifying casualties, while a massive attack in Champagne, involving two French armies, ground to a halt with the loss of 145,000 men.

CROSS-REFERENCE YPRES: PAGES 32–33

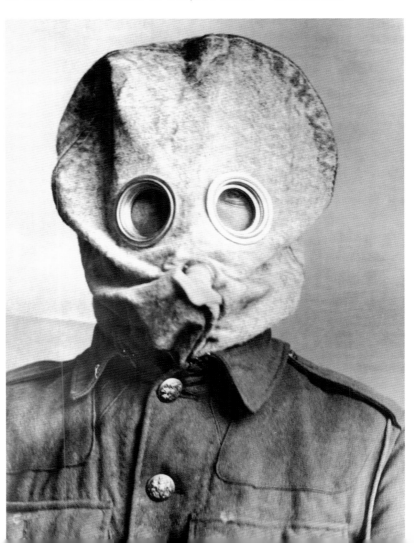

Men into monsters: early gas masks were not only hideous-looking but also extremely cumbersome.

First Zeppelin Raid on London

Until May 31, 1915, the citizens of London had known the Great War as something that happened elsewhere—in France, at sea, in Russia, and the Middle East. On May 31, though, the war came to them. A huge Zeppelin airship raid flew slowly over the capital, dropped its load of bombs and disappeared over the horizon.

Bombing was a new aspect of total war. Seeking victory, each side needed to use all its resources in the war effort: ships, factories, workers, railways, and mines. Women played a vital role, doing jobs previously done only by men, and governments controlled labor and supplies. As everyone and everything was geared to the war effort, all were a legitimate target for the bombers. There was no longer just a battle front, there was now a home front as well.

NEW WARFARE

The use of aircraft changed warfare. At first, as we saw at the Battle of the Marne, planes were used simply for

Death from the sky

"[The bombs] had simply destroyed the road down which I walked and there were bits of bodies all over and whole bodies and heads and arms and legs, **bits blown into trees**, just everywhere and nobody about, there wasn't any organization at all, it was pathetic."

Frieda Sawden recalls the ghastly carnage caused by a Zeppelin raid on Hull in 1915. Quoted in Richard van Emden and Steve Humphries, *All Quiet on the Home Front* (Headline, 2003).

Enemy above! A German Zeppelin airship over Yarmouth uses its searchlight to select a suitable target.

Deadly load: a 220-pound (100-kg) bomb is attached beneath a German Gotha bomber.

TIMELINE

WAR IN THE AIR 1914–1918

August 14, 1914 ▶ French carry out first ever bombing raid, hitting German Zeppelin airship hangars.

October 5, 1914 ▶ A French Voisin III shoots down a German Aviatik B1, the first time one plane had shot down another.

March 21, 1915 ▶ First air raid on Paris by a Zeppelin airship leaves 23 people dead.

May 31, 1915 ▶ First air raid on London by a Zeppelin airship.

June 7, 1915 ▶ The usefulness of Zeppelin airships declines after a high-flying enemy fighter downs the first one.

May 23, 1917 ▶ 21 German Gotha bombers kill 95 people in a raid on the British port of Folkestone.

April 21, 1918 ▶ Manfred von Richthofen (the "Red Baron"), the greatest fighter ace of the war, is killed in action over the Somme.

observation. Then other planes attempted to shoot them down, so the fighter aircraft was born. One-to-one duels between fighter pilots—known as "aces" or "knights of the air"—were one of the few glamorous aspects of the war. More important were air attacks on military and industrial targets. In 1917, the British began using ground-attack aircraft to support infantry assaults, a tactic that both sides used to break the deadlock of trench warfare in 1918. The massed Allied assaults during that summer, combining troops, tanks, artillery, and aircraft, foreshadowed the famous *Blitzkrieg* tactics of World War II.

BOMBERS

Equally important was the development of long-range bombing. The Russians led with the Sikorsky Ilya Mourometz, the world's first four-engine bomber. In 1914, its seven-man crew could fly 400 miles (644 km) at about 75 mph (120 kph) with a 1,540-pound (700-kg) bomb load. Four years later, the Handley Page V 1500, with 4,990 pounds (2,268 kg) of bombs, could reach Berlin from behind the British lines, and complete a return journey of some 1,000 miles (1,600 km).

CROSS-REFERENCE ATTACKS OF 1917 AND 1918: PAGES 32–33, 38–41

Allies Land in Gallipoli

Australian troops watch the unloading of a 6-inch (150-mm) howitzer at Anzac Cove.

In a daring seaborne landing, on April 25, 1915, an Allied force of about 52,000 men landed on the Turkish-held Gallipoli Peninsula. The plan was to seize the peninsula and gain control of the Dardanelles, the narrow seaway linking the Black Sea to the Mediterranean. This would allow the Allies to capture Constantinople (now Istanbul), link up with southern Russia, and, perhaps, knock Turkey out of the war, also opening up a new front against the Central Powers of Germany and Austria-Hungary.

DARDANELLES DISASTER

The operation was a disaster. After failing to take advantage of their surprise attack, the French, British, and Anzac (Australian and New Zealand Army Corps) troops were pinned down by well-organized Turkish resistance. Despite thousands of reinforcements and a second

Australian misery

"In an old Australian homestead with roses round the door
A girl received a letter from a far and distant shore.
With her mother's arms around her 'neath the blue Australian skies
She slowly read the letter and the tears fell from her eyes.
'Why do I weep? Why do I pray?
My love's asleep so far away
He played his part that Autumn day
And left my heart on Suvla Bay.'"

An Australian song commemorating Anzac sacrifices during the second Gallipoli landing, at Suvla Bay. Quoted in Lyn Macdonald, *1914–1918 Voices and Images of the Great War* (Penguin, 1991).

THE TURKISH FRONTS 1914–1918

November 1, 1914	▶ Turkey joins the war on the side of the Central Powers.
November 6, 1914	▶ Anglo-Indian force lands in Turkish province of Mesopotamia, taking Basra on November 22.
January 14, 1915	▶ Advancing into Persia, Russians take Tabriz in a drive to link up with the British to their south.
April 25, 1915	▶ Combined forces of French, British, and Anzacs land on the Turkish Gallipoli Peninsula.
May 25, 1915	▶ Beginning of the worst phase of the Turkish massacre of perhaps a million Armenians.
April 29, 1916	▶ Surrounded Anglo-Indian force in Kut surrenders to the Turks.
March 11, 1917	▶ Tide begins turning in the Middle East as an Anglo-Indian force occupies Baghdad.
April 25, 1918	▶ Turks take Kars during a rapid advance into Russia.

landing in August, the Allies were still unable to break the deadlock. When the men were finally withdrawn early the following year, the Allies had suffered almost 250,000 casualties—about half the total number of troops landed at Gallipoli.

TURKEY'S WAR

The Turkish Empire entered the war on the side of the Central Powers on November 1, 1914. This immediately meant it had to fight on a number of difficult fronts. Beside the Gallipoli assault, it faced a massive Russian attack through the region of Armenia, between the Black Sea and Lake Van. It also had troops combating an Anglo-Russian invasion of Persia (now Iran), further Russian attacks through Azerbaijan, and an Anglo-Indian invasion of Mesopotamia (now Iraq) up the Euphrates River. Later, it also had to deal with a British-backed Arab revolt.

Given their comparative economic weakness, the Turks fared remarkably well. As we have seen, the Gallipoli landings were thwarted, and in 1916, the Anglo-Indian force in Mesopotamia was surrounded in Kut and forced to surrender. Along the northern frontiers, after years of costly fighting, by 1918, the Russians were in headlong retreat. Tragically, however, Turkish Armenians in the region were subjected to a horrific massacre of about a million people. Further east, the Turkish forces were unable to prevent the Russians and British from gaining control over Persia and its crucial oil fields.

Fleeing for their lives: Armenians try to escape the worst civilian massacre of the war.

CROSS-REFERENCE WAR IN THE MIDDLE EAST: PAGES 34–35

Sinking of the *Lusitania*

7 MAY 1915

On the afternoon of May 7, 1915, the transatlantic liner SS *Lusitania* was torpedoed 14 miles (22.5 km) off the Irish coast. She sank in 18 minutes. About 1,200 lives were lost, including 128 Americans and 3 Germans. The incident caused an international outcry.

Germany, whose U-20 submarine had fired the torpedo, claimed the ship had been a legitimate target as it was listed as an "armed cruiser" (it was indeed fitted with gun mountings) and carried armaments (some 5,000 U.S.-made artillery shells). The British condemned the sinking as a typical example of Germany's cowardly submarine tactics. In the U.S., then still neutral, public opinion turned against the Central Powers. Nevertheless, the U.S. did not join the Allies for two more years.

BATTLE OF THE BLOCKADES

All the major powers involved in World War I were trading nations, none more so than Britain. Their people and industries needed imports such as sugar, rubber, and oil. As all freight came by sea, the Allies and the Central Powers did their best to disrupt the other's shipping.

From November 1914, Britain used its immense Royal Navy to blockade Germany. All ships going to a continental port were stopped and searched, and cargoes bound for Germany were confiscated. The blockade was successful—by 1915, German imports had fallen by 55 percent. Experts reckon that by the end of the war 763,000 people had died of starvation because of the blockade. Essentially, the war ended because Germany's starving civilians had lost the will to fight.

CONVOYS

Germany had retaliated with a campaign of submarine warfare against British ships and sometimes against neutrals trading with Britain. By February 1917, 230 supply ships a month were being sunk and Britain

Deaths that shocked America: the mass grave of some of those who died when a German U-boat torpedoed the SS Lusitania, 1915.

CROSS-REFERENCE
WAR AT SEA:
PAGES 24–25
AMERICA'S ENTRY
INTO THE WAR:
PAGES 30–31

TIMELINE

THE TWO BLOCKADES 1914–1917

November 3, 1914
▶ Britain declares the North Sea to be a British military area, claiming the right to prevent any supplies from reaching Germany.

January 1, 1915
▶ Germany introduces rationing.

February 18, 1915
▶ Germany announces that it will target all shipping in the "war zone" around Britain.

September 1, 1915
▶ Germany suspends unrestricted submarine warfare in the face of international protest.

July 1, 1916
▶ German U-boat fleet totals 100 vessels.

February 1, 1917
▶ Germany reintroduces unrestricted submarine warfare.

May 10, 1917
▶ A convoy system is introduced for Allied merchant shipping in the Atlantic.

December 31, 1917
▶ Britain rations sugar, the first of several foods to be rationed before the end of the war.

was in dire straits. The following month, over half a million tons of shipping were sunk. After that, the situation improved. The British harvest was the best ever and by gathering ships into convoys, the Royal Navy was better protected from the German submarines.

A new dimension of warfare: submarines, such as this German U-boat, changed naval warfare for ever.

Changes in the size of the world's major merchant fleets, 1914–1918

Reductions in size were almost exclusively due to enemy action.

Country	1914 tonnage (millions)	1918 tonnage (millions)
Austria-Hungary	1.05	0.71
Britain	18.89	16.34
France	1.92	1.96
Germany	5.13	3.25
Italy	1.43	1.24
Japan	1.70	2.32
Turkey	0.11	0.09
U.S.	9.45	16.95

Italy Enters the War

23 May 1915

Mountain warfare: Italian troops at Trentino, 1915.

To the fury of the German high command, when war broke out in 1914, the Italian government declared itself neutral. As it coveted Trieste and other Austro-Hungarian areas, this was not so surprising. On May 23, 1915, following a secret treaty with the Allies in London, the Italians joined the war on their side. They had been promised territory in the Trieste region and immediately set about trying to seize it.

The road to Trieste was much rougher than the Italians anticipated. First they had to cross the Isonzo River and fight a series of exhausting battles there throughout 1915 and 1916. Four offensives during 1915, all known as Battles of Isonzo, cost the Italians almost 250,000 casualties for few gains. The following year, after yet another Italian attack around the Isonzo River had failed, the Austro-Hungarians launched their own offensive. Further west, around Asiago, they headed toward the cities of Padua and Venice. The move came as a complete surprise and was halted only after the loss of another 147,000 Italian troops. By late summer, the Italians had moved men back to the Isonzo to renew their offensives.

CAPORETTO

In 1917, the Italians came close to total defeat. In May and June, they concentrated their forces for two further offensives on the Isonzo and Asiago fronts. The Austro-Hungarians, reinforced by German divisions, noticed how weak this left the enemy line around Caporetto and, on October 24, launched a massive attack there. Breakthrough was immediate. Within three weeks,

TIMELINE

THE AUSTRO-ITALIAN FRONT 1915–1918

April 26, 1915 ▶ At the secret Treaty of London, Italy agrees to join the Allies in return for Austrian territory around the Gulf of Venice.

May 23, 1915 ▶ Italy enters the war on the Allied side, breaking links with the countries of the Triple Alliance.

June 23, 1915 ▶ The Italians launch their first attack toward the port of Trieste—the First Battle of Isonzo.

May 15, 1916 ▶ Austro-Hungarian commander von Hötzendorf launches the Battle of Asiago, a surprise attack in the Trentino region.

May 12, 1917 ▶ Start of the Tenth Battle of Isonzo in which the Italians fail to break through.

October 24, 1917 ▶ Beginning of the Battle of Caporetto, a massive defeat for the Italians.

October 24, 1918 ▶ Final Italian offensive and the Austro-Hungarians flee.

November 3, 1918 ▶ Terms agreed for a ceasefire on the Italian front.

the Italians had withdrawn to the torrential Piave River, only 20 miles (32 km) from Venice. They suffered huge losses.

THE TIDE TURNS

Reinforced by British and French divisions, the Italians clung on in the summer of 1918, when the Austro-Hungarian army was swelled by troops from the victorious Russian front. Just before the end of the war, the Italian army went on the offensive again. It made spectacular progress against a disheartened enemy until peace terms were agreed in November.

CROSS-REFERENCE DEFEAT OF RUSSIA: PAGES 36–37

Despair and humiliation: Italian troops in retreat after the Battle of Caporetto.

Caporetto: Austria-Hungary's greatest triumph

The sides: Along the Isonzo Front, 41 Italian divisions faced 35 Austro-Hungarian.

Where: The Austro-Hungarians attacked through Caporetto, a town in the bend of the Isonzo River.

How: After a five-hour gas and artillery bombardment, the Austro-Hungarian attack came in mountain fog.

Progress: The Austro-Hungarians advanced 14 miles (22.5 km) on the first day, 70 miles (113 km) in all.

Losses: The Italians lost 2,500 guns, some 30,000 casualties, and 250,000 men taken prisoner.

Battle of Verdun Begins

The longest and costliest battle of the war began on February 21, 1916, with a 1-million-shell bombardment of the French fortifications around the ancient city of Verdun in eastern France. The Allies were taken by surprise. They had been planning enormous and simultaneous French, British, and Russian summer attacks in 1916 but the German commander-in-chief, von Falkenhayn, struck first. His aim was to "bleed France white"—attacking a town he knew the French would never surrender, he hoped to produce a mincing machine that would crush their army.

PÉTAIN

The plan started well. As 1 million men swept forward, after only four days the great fort of Douaumont fell. The following day, the inspirational General Pétain was put in charge of Verdun's defense and the French Second Army began to take up positions there. Pétain reorganized the French artillery, rotated the men on the front line to cut exhaustion, and opened the "Sacred Way" road for bringing food, water, and ammunition to the front line. The French watchword was, *Ils ne passeront pas!*— "They will not get through!"

Living with the dead

"**I sent out several reconnoitring parties. None of them returned. . . . I had no further communication with Headquarters. Ammunition and food had . . . run short . . . [and] I had nothing to eat or drink. Hunger made me unsteady on my feet . . . looking round me, a terrifying thought took hold of me: we were separated from the living.**"

A French lieutenant remembers the Verdun experience, May 1916. Quoted in David Mason, *Verdun* (Windrush Press, 2000).

The horror of war: a mound of human bones uncovered after the terrible slaughter at Verdun, 1916.

TIMELINE

THE HELL OF VERDUN 1915–1916

December 6, 1915 ▶ Allied conference at Chantilly agrees on a concerted attack on all fronts the following summer.

February 21, 1915 ▶ German assault on Verdun begins with a huge artillery barrage.

June 4, 1916 ▶ Russian General Brusilov brings forward his offensive on the Eastern Front to help France.

June 7, 1916 ▶ Germans renew their Verdun offensive; Fort Vaux falls.

July 1, 1916 ▶ Anglo-French offensive on the Somme begins early to take the pressure off Verdun.

August 28, 1916 ▶ Hindenburg replaces Falkenhayn as German commander-in-chief.

December 15, 1916 ▶ Last French offensive at Verdun begins, returning the front line to where it had been in February.

December 26, 1916 ▶ Nivelle replaces Joffre as French commander-in-chief.

ALLIES TO THE RESCUE

Despite Pétain's efforts, the German advance ground forward, sucking more and more French troops into the maelstrom. An attempt to recapture Fort Douaumont failed in May. Within a month, the Germans had seized Mort Homme (Dead Man) Hill and the mighty Fort Vaux. Finally, on June 22, the German artillery and infantry attacked Fort Souville, the last major fortress before Verdun itself.

Eleven days later, Falkenhayn was forced to postpone his offensive because German resources had become dangerously overstretched. As well as attacking Verdun, they were needed to counter a Russian offensive against Austria-Hungary and an Anglo-French offensive on the Somme River. The Battle of Verdun was now at its turning point. The town did not fall, and over the coming months, French counterattacks gradually and painfully recaptured nearly all the ground surrendered earlier. When the fighting eventually stopped, at Christmas, the two armies had lost almost a million men, 434,000 Germans and 542,000 French. France had not exactly been bled white but its health was far from robust.

Fighting over this? The ruins of the town of Verdun after it had been fought over for almost an entire year.

CROSS-REFERENCE **RUSSIAN OFFENSIVE 1916:** PAGES 26–27 **SOMME OFFENSIVE:** PAGES 28–29

Battle of Jutland Begins

For the first two years of the war, the German High Seas Fleet did not live up to its name: it remained in Wilhelmshaven harbor, secure behind its minefields and torpedo nets. Suddenly, on the morning of May 31, 1916, it upped anchor and steamed into the North Sea. Its plan, framed by Admiral Scheer, was to lure part of the British Grand Fleet and sink it before it could be reinforced.

SHARED VICTORY

At first, the plan went well. Intercepting coded German wireless signals, the British fleet sailed to meet the enemy. Admiral Beatty's battlecruisers, 60 miles (96 km) ahead of the rest, encountered the Germans on the afternoon of May 31. After suffering surprising losses, Beatty suddenly found himself face-to-face with the main German fleet. He promptly turned, luring the High Seas Fleet toward the much larger Grand Fleet. The two came within range in the early evening. After a sharp encounter, Scheer turned about and escaped into the gathering gloom. The next day, the German fleet was safely back in Wilhelmshaven, where it remained until surrender in 1918. Having lost fewer ships, the Germans claimed victory, while the British regarded the Battle of Jutland as a tactical victory since they controlled the seas for the rest of the war.

MINOR BATTLES

The Jutland encounter was the only major surface battle of the war. The Germans concentrated on submarine warfare, leaving the Royal Navy in command on the surface. In the first battle of the war, three German cruisers had been sunk off the Heligoland Bight (August 28, 1914). Three months later, the Royal Navy lost two old armored cruisers to a much larger German force off South America.

Full steam ahead: German Dreadnought battleships, part of a fleet that Winston Churchill had criticized as an "expensive luxury."

August 28, 1914 ▶ First naval encounter of the war sees German losses at the Battle of the Heligoland Bight in the North Sea.

November 1, 1914 ▶ Serious misunderstanding leads to the destruction of Rear-Admiral Craddock's force at the Battle of Coronel.

December 8, 1914 ▶ At the Battle of the Falkland Islands, the Germans lose some 2,000 men and four warships.

January 24, 1915 ▶ German raiders in the North Sea surprised at the Battle of Dogger Bank.

May 31, 1916 ▶ Battle of Jutland sees a tactical British victory but at a heavy price.

November 21, 1918 ▶ German High Seas Fleet surrenders.

June 21, 1919 ▶ Germans scuttle their High Seas Fleet in Scapa Flow, the British naval base.

The following January, a far superior British force tracked down the German raiders near the Falkland Islands and sank all but one of them. The escapee was scuttled shortly afterward, leaving Britain ruling the world's waves. Allied naval superiority was confirmed at the Battle of the Dogger Bank, when a German scouting group was scattered with the loss of one of its battlecruisers.

CROSS-REFERENCE
SUBMARINE
WARFARE: PAGES
18–19

British soldiers watch as the German cruiser Mainz *is hit by gunfire at the Battle of Heligoland Bight.*

Ships present and lost at Battle of Jutland

(figures in brackets are losses)

	Dreadnoughts	Battlecruisers	Cruisers	Destroyers
British Grand Fleet				
	28 (0)	9 (3)	34 (3)	77 (8)
Men lost: 6,784				
German High Seas Fleet				
	16 + 6 old	5 (1)	11 (4)	61 (5)
				(1 old)
Men lost: 3,099				

Brusilov Offensive Begins

General Alexei Brusilov, the most capable Russian commander in World War I, who went on to serve in the Communist Red Army.

General Alexei Brusilov (1853–1926) was the most competent high-ranking Russian officer serving on the Eastern Front during World War I. Certainly the attack that he launched in the southwest against Austro-Hungarian and German forces on June 4, 1916, was better organized than any other Russian offensive. At first it met with great success. By late June, several Russian units had advanced 60 miles (96 km) and some 350,000 prisoners, mostly Austrian, had been taken.

Brusilov's triumph was deceptive. At Verdun and on the Italian Front, Russia's allies had been under serious pressure in early 1917. Responding to this, the Russian armies had planned to attack right along the front, from Lithuania in the north to the Carpathian Mountains in the south. As it happened, only Brusilov's forces had been ready for the assault. It came as little surprise, therefore, when his breakthrough was not followed up.

CRISIS

In some places, the Russian advance stopped after just two weeks. The main problem was not enemy resistance so much as lack of supply. Guns ran out of shells. Soldiers ran out of almost everything: rifles, bullets, and, most important of all, food and water. Under the strain of supplying the armies, the Russian railway system had all but collapsed. Engines were not serviced and broke down, blocking the track. The track itself was poorly maintained and sometimes even unusable.

Undaunted, Brusilov attacked again in July but had to call a halt when his ammunition dumps ran empty. Meanwhile, the Germans and Austrians brought up reinforcements. Hindenburg took command of all the Central Powers' forces and soon stabilized the front. By the autumn, having lost another million men, Russia was in crisis.

TIMELINE	**THE EASTERN FRONT 1916–1917**
March 17, 1916	▶ Russian attack toward Vilna called off after one week's disastrous casualties.
June 4, 1916	▶ Brusilov offensive begins in the southwest sector of the Eastern Front.
June 7, 1916	▶ Advancing Russian forces take the town of Lutsk, a significant gain.
June 16, 1916	▶ A counteroffensive by Germany in the north halts the Russian advance there.
June 17, 1916	▶ Russians seize Czernowitz on the southern front, a significant gain.
September 20, 1916	▶ Last Russian attempt to advance fails.
February 27, 1917	▶ The city of Petrograd dissolves into chaos as strikers and mutinying troops fill the streets.
March 2, 1917	▶ Revolution in Russia—Tsar Nicholas II is forced to abdicate, March 15.

A changed man

"His Majesty is a changed man. . . . He is no longer seriously interested in anything. . . . **One can't rule an empire and command an army in the field** in this manner. If he doesn't realize it in time, something catastrophic is bound to happen."

Paul Benckendorff, the Grand Marshal of the Court, complains privately about Tsar Nicholas, autumn of 1916. Quoted in Dominic Lieven, *Nicholas II* (John Murray, 1993).

REVOLUTION

During the winter of 1916–1917, the Russian Army disintegrated fast. Morale sank beyond repair. Officers lost their authority. Hundreds of thousands of troops abandoned their positions and went home. Meanwhile, back in the cities, strikes paralysed industry and the streets filled with protesters. Finally, in March 1917, Tsar Nicholas abdicated. This revolution produced an unelected, liberal-minded Provisional Government. Immediately, however, it made a disastrous decision—to continue with the war.

CROSS-REFERENCE
IMPACT OF THE WAR ON RUSSIA: PAGES 36–37

Morale at rock bottom: Russian soldiers surrender en masse in Galicia, 1917.

Battle of the Somme Begins

The third Allied attempt to take the pressure off the French began on June 24, 1916, with a British bombardment of the German lines above the Somme River in northern France. By July 1, when the attack began, the Allies had fired more than 1.5 million shells. Many, particularly from the heavy guns, had failed to explode. Even so, the Germans knew that an infantry attack was due.

The Battle of the Somme began at 7.30 a.m. on July 1, 1916. Around 58,000 men were lost on the first day and although attacks continued into the autumn, no breakthrough was achieved.

MIXED CONSEQUENCES

The bungling on the Somme has often been criticized. The battleground was chosen not for strategic reasons but largely because it was where the French and British armies met, making a combined attack easier. The Germans had been digging in there since 1914, so their positions were well prepared. The artillery barrage was poorly conducted. The inexperienced troops—mostly from the new volunteer army—were put at unnecessary risk.

While the losses shocked the British, they were similar to those of other nations. When the offensive was halted in mid-November, the British had lost 419,000, the French 194,451, and the Germans 650,000. The German losses helped save Verdun from capture and heavily influenced the German decision to fall back to the Hindenburg Line in March 1917 and thereafter fight a largely defensive war.

Living among the dead: a British trench on the Somme, 1916.

THE SOMME AND ITS AFTERMATH 1916–1917

June 24, 1916	Eight-day Somme artillery barrage begins.
July 1, 1916	Battle of the Somme begins with a massive infantry assault that is only partly successful.
July 15, 1916	British troops take High Wood but the opportunity for a breakthrough is missed. South African forces seize Delville Wood and hold out heroically for six days.
September 15, 1916	Tanks first used in battle, causing widespread terror in the German lines.
November 18, 1916	Somme offensive halted after Allies gain a maximum of 6 miles (10 km).
March 14, 1917	German Army begins withdrawal to the pre-prepared Hindenburg defensive line.

A British Mark I tank at the Somme. Although not well used at first, tanks would eventually prove a decisive weapon.

CROSS-REFERENCE
BATTLE OF VERDUN: PAGES **22–23**
HINDENBURG LINE: PAGES **32–33**

The colonial and imperial sacrifice

Both Britain and France relied heavily on troops from their worldwide empires, many of whom fought on the Somme.

- Approximately 2 million troops from the French African colonies served in the war. Over 200,000 were killed and perhaps three times that number wounded.
- Approximately 2.5 million British colonial and dominion troops served in the war. The casualties were as follows:
    - almost 60,000 Canadians killed and 149,000 wounded
    - over 53,000 Australians killed and 155,000 wounded
    - over 62,000 Indians killed and 66,000 wounded
    - about 16,000 New Zealanders killed and 41,000 wounded.

U.S. Enters the War

"Your support, please": President Woodrow Wilson asks Congress to declare war on Germany, April 1917.

When war broke out between the European Powers in 1914, the U.S. was strictly neutral. The Old World, so the saying went, could "stew in its own juice." President Wilson was re-elected in 1916 on the slogan "He kept us out of the war."

END OF NEUTRALITY

The policy of neutrality was sorely tested. Anglo-American ties ran deep. The U.S.'s trade with the Allies was worth $3.2 billion in 1916 and as they also owed U.S. bankers $2.5 billion, victory by the Central Powers would have spelled financial disaster. On top of that came U.S. anger at Germany's unrestricted submarine warfare.

Then, in February 1917, Britain made public an intercepted German telegram. It was to the Mexican government and suggested that if Mexico joined the war on Germany's side, it could invade the U.S. to recapture territory that had once been Mexican! Stating that it was America's duty to keep the world safe for democracy, in April American President Wilson asked Congress for a declaration of war. It duly obliged on April 6.

THE AMERICAN EXPEDITIONARY FORCE

The U.S. was not prepared for total war. Its army was small, its air force tiny, and its navy untested. However, in a few months it had mustered all its might behind the war effort.

For example, its air force, numbering 55 planes when war was declared, rose to 3,227 planes in 1918. Over the same period the army swelled from 175,000 to some 6 million, of whom about 2 million served overseas.

John J. Pershing, the only American general with much wartime experience, was given the task of producing an American Expeditionary

Force (AEF) capable of influencing the outcome on the Western Front. His first troops reached France in October 1917. By May 1918, the AEF was strong enough to play an important part in halting the German offensive at Château-Thierry. Similar examples of brave resistance followed. When the Allied offensive began in the summer, the AEF again distinguished itself at St. Mihiel. After suffering terrible casualties in the Argonne Forest, it was back in the front line when the fighting stopped on November 11.

CROSS-REFERENCE FINAL BREACH OF THE HINDENBURG LINE: PAGES 40–41

Allies united: U.S. soldiers, wearing British-style helmets, fire a French gun on the Western Front, 1918.

Champions of the rights of mankind

"The world must be made safe for democracy. . . . We have no selfish ends to serve. We desire no conquest, no dominion. We seek no indemnities for ourselves, no material compensation for the sacrifices we shall freely make. We are but one of the champions of the rights of mankind."

President Wilson's speech to Congress asking for war, April 2, 1917. Quoted in www.lib.byu.edu/ ~rdh/wwi/1917/wilswarm.html

Third Battle of Ypres Begins

Since the Somme campaign had ground to a halt at the end of 1916, Britain's Field Marshal Haig had been planning another offensive that would finally achieve breakthrough on the Western Front. He put his plan into operation on July 31, 1917, striking out of the Ypres salient.

BLOODY NECESSITY?

As so often on the Western Front, the enemy knew the attack was coming. Occupying higher ground, which they had been reinforcing for the past year, the Germans had seen the preparations. They had also been warned by the Allied capture of Messines Ridge in June and by the heaviest artillery and aircraft barrage of the war. The first attack, striking northeast, advanced 1.9 miles (3 km). Progress to the south was slower but by October the British had finally reached the Ypres Ridge, the high ground that dominated the salient.

Against much advice, Field Marshal Haig pressed on until the village of Passchendaele was in Allied hands on November 6. The offensive had cost 310,000 casualties and gained no more than 6 miles (10 km) of ground. Notwithstanding the slaughter for so little gain, it may be argued that the battle had been necessary because of the poor state of the French forces farther south.

MUTINY

Despite the recent bloodbath at Verdun, the French planned to mark 1917 with a fresh offensive. The first plans fizzled out when, in March, the Germans suddenly shortened their front line by withdrawing to the Hindenburg Line (which the Germans named the Siegfried Line) of concrete bunkers, barbed wire, tunnels, machine gun emplacements, and trenches. Undaunted, after the British had diverted German attention with an attack at Arras, the French general Nivelle launched his Aisne Offensive on April 16.

The French advanced along a 50-mile (80-km) front, employing 1.2 million men and 7,000 guns. There were some notable gains, including seizure of part

Dead end: Canadian machine gunners before the shattered village of Passchendaele, November 1917.

TIMELINE | THE WESTERN FRONT 1917

March 5, 1917 ▶ German forces begin their withdrawal to the Hindenburg (Siegfried) Line.

April 9, 1917 ▶ Canadian capture of Vimy Ridge, the highlight of the British attack at Arras.

April 16, 1917 ▶ General Nivelle launches disastrous French offensive on the Aisne River.

April 29, 1917 ▶ First of over 100 mutinies in the French Army, with troops refusing to attack.

May 15, 1917 ▶ General Nivelle replaced by General Pétain.

June 7, 1917 ▶ Careful planning allows the British to capture Messines Ridge, southeast of Ypres.

June 31, 1917 ▶ Britain's Field Marshal Haig launches the Third Battle of Ypres, which ends in the mud of Passchendaele.

November 20, 1917 ▶ British break through German lines at Cambrai.

General Nivelle's orders to advance led to widespread mutinies among French troops.

of the Hindenburg Line but no breakthrough. By the end of the month, alarming signs began to appear in the French ranks: some of the battle-hardened *poilus* (French footsoldiers) refused to take part in any more attacks. Had the Germans known and been able to target the mutinous units, they might have ended the war a year earlier.

CROSS-REFERENCE FINAL BREACH OF THE HINDENBURG LINE: PAGES 40–41 ▶

Mown down

"**Our opponents were fighting a rearguard action which resulted in a massacre for both sides. Our boys were falling like ninepins,** but it was even worse for them. If they stood up to surrender they were mown down by their own machine-gun fire aimed from the rear at us; if they leapfrogged back they were caught in our barrage."

Corporal H. C. Baker of the Canadian Expeditionary Force, November 1917. Quoted in Lyn Macdonald, *They Called It Passchendaele* (Penguin, 1993).

Russia Signs Treaty of Brest-Litovsk

The abdication of Tsar Nicholas II in March 1917 did little to help Russia's war effort. Much of the country's infrastructure had collapsed, millions were starving and increasing numbers looked to extremist groups for salvation. Among these, one of the better organized was a Communist sect known as the Bolsheviks. Its members were in the soviet (committee) set up in February 1917 by Petrograd socialists as an alternative administration.

PROVISIONAL GOVERNMENT

The Provisional Government under Prince Lvov wanted Russia to have a Western-style democracy, similar to Britain and France. Understandably, these countries pressured the Provisional Government to stay in the war. Alexander Kerensky, Russia's dynamic Minister of War, gambled on military victory to please his allies and raise morale at home. Russia's last desperate offensive (known as the Kerensky Offensive), led by the ever-willing General Brusilov, was launched against the Austro-Hungarians on June 18, 1917.

The outcome of the Kerensky Offensive was all too predictable. After some quick gains, the Russians collapsed in the face of a German counteroffensive. By August 21, German forces had taken the Baltic port of Riga, opening the road to the city of Petrograd (now St. Petersburg). At this point the Bolshevik-inspired Red Guards saved the government from a military coup by General Kornilov. On October 24–25, the Bolsheviks themselves struck, seizing power in Petrograd.

THE COMMUNIST PEACE

The Bolsheviks, led by Vladimir Lenin and Leon Trotsky, gradually spread their Communist revolution across Russia. As they had promised to bring peace, Foreign Minister Trotsky signed an armistice with the Germans in December. He would not agree full peace terms, however, as he hoped the Communist revolution would spread from Russia into Germany. The Germans lost patience and in February, launched an offensive that brought them even closer to Petrograd.

Alexander Kerensky (in the car) salutes Russian troops asked to undertake one last futile offensive.

TIMELINE

COLLAPSE AND REVOLUTION IN RUSSIA 1917–1918*

February 27, 1917 ▶ Socialists form the Petrograd Soviet as an alternative administration in the city and beyond.

April 3, 1917 ▶ With tacit German approval, the Bolshevik leader Lenin arrives in Petrograd from Switzerland.

June 18, 1917 ▶ War Minister Kerensky launches his summer offensive in the southwest.

July 5, 1917 ▶ Counteroffensive by Germany soon has Russian army in rapid retreat.

October 24–25, 1917 ▶ Bolshevik Revolution in Petrograd topples the Provisional Government.

December 2, 1917 ▶ Bolsheviks sign a formal armistice with Germany and Austria-Hungary.

February 18, 1918 ▶ German advance threatens Petrograd, forcing Trotsky to agree terms.

March 3, 1918 ▶ Russia accepts terms of the Treaty of Brest-Litovsk.

*As Russia used a slightly different calendar before the Revolution, different dates are sometimes given for the same event.

Conspiracy against Communism?

"On February 21, we received new terms from Germany. . . . All of us, including Lenin, were of the impression that the Germans had come to an agreement with the Allies about crushing the Soviets. . . . On March 3, our delegation signed the peace treaty without even reading it . . . the Brest-Litovsk peace was like the hangman's noose."

From Leon Trotsky's autobiography, *My Life*. Quoted in www.spartacus.schoolnet.co.uk/FWWbrest.htm

The Bolsheviks now had no choice but to sign whatever terms the Germans dictated. By the humiliating Treaty of Brest-Litovsk, the Russian frontier was moved 250 miles (400 km) farther east from what had been agreed in December. Russia lost the Ukraine, Poland, the Baltic Provinces, and almost all territory gained over the previous 200 years. With it went a high proportion of the country's mining and industry. The German victory was total.

CROSS-REFERENCE RUSSIA: PAGES 8–9, 26–27

"Revolution comrades!" Bolshevik leader Lenin addresses a crowd of workers in Petrograd (St. Petersburg), 1917.

German Spring Offensive Begins

21 MARCH 1918

In contrast to 1917, in January 1918, the Allied commanders on the Western Front were planning to strengthen their defenses while the Germans were organizing a huge offensive. General Ludendorff knew that with Russia neutralized and U.S. forces not yet in Europe in numbers, he had a unique opportunity for a decisive move. His plan was to put Germany into a strong position for a negotiated peace.

SOMME BREAKTHROUGH

Ludendorff's principal aim was to break the British and Belgian forces around Ypres and seize the Channel ports. He began on March 21, trying to split the French from the British by sending 63 divisions against the 26 British divisions defending the Somme area. After an intense and precise bombardment, Ludendorff's troops routed the British and advanced much farther than expected.

German troops smash through the British front line during the 1918 Spring Offensive.

Wartime losses of major combatants

NB In many cases the figures are estimates.

Country	Population (millions)	Numbers in forces (millions)	Killed and missing	Wounded	Civilian deaths
Austria-Hungary	49.9	7.8	539,630	1,943,240	unknown
Belgium	7.52	0.27	38,170	44,690	30,000
Bulgaria	5.5	1.2	77,450	152,400	275,000
France	39.6	8.66	1,385,300	4,329,200	40,000
Germany	67	13.4	2,037,000	5,687,000	700,000
Italy	35	5.9	462,400	955,000	unknown
Russia	167	12	1,800,000	4,950,000	2,000,000
Serbia	5	0.71	127,500	133,150	600,000
Turkey	21.3	0.99	236,000	770,000	2,000,000
UK	46.4	5.7	702,410	1,662,625	1,386
U.S.	92	4.35	51,822	230,074	–

TIMELINE	THE WESTERN FRONT MARCH–JULY 1918
March 21, 1918	With Russia neutralized and few U.S. troops ready for battle, Germany launches its Spring Offensive on the Somme.
April 9, 1918	General Ludendorff begins Phase 2 of the German Spring Offensive, aimed at his main target, the British in Flanders.
April 11, 1918	With his forces stretched to breaking point, Field Marshal Haig gives his famous order, "There must be no retirement."
May 27, 1918	The Third Battle of the River Aisne begins the third phase of the Spring Offensive.
June 9, 1918	A second German attack in the Aisne region fails to break through.
July 15, 1918	Ludendorff launches the fifth and final phase of his offensive with attacks around Rheims.
July 18, 1918	Vast Allied counterattack on the Marne ends German Spring Offensive.

After the Somme attack had run out of steam, on April 9, Ludendorff began his principal attack south of Ypres. Swift initial gains were made against British, Portuguese (now with the Allies), and Belgian troops. However, although the Allied line bent, it did not break.

The next month, to draw reinforcements from Flanders, the Germans attacked the French on the Aisne River. They progressed 12 miles (20 km) on the first day, the biggest advance since 1914. However, as on the Somme, Ludendorff pressed on farther than planned and his forces became overstretched. His advance was stopped by early June, with U.S. help.

Yanks to the rescue: U.S. machine gunners helping to halt the dramatic German offensive of spring, 1918.

LAST CHANCE

Still delaying the Flanders push, in June, Ludendorff began an offensive farther south, in the Noyon-Montdiddier region. It made little headway against Allies who now used deep defensive formations. The final Spring Offensive began in mid-July and comprised attacks on either side of Rheims. Although the Germans did manage to cross the Marne River below the city, the attack was checked by French, British, Italian, and U.S. units.

This was the moment supreme Allied commander, Marshal Foch, had been waiting for. Seeing the enemy exhausted and depleted, on July 18, he ordered a substantial counterattack.

CROSS-REFERENCE
RUSSIA'S DEFEAT: PAGES 36–37
ALLIED OFFENSIVE: PAGES 40–41

"Black Day of the German Army"

Some three weeks after the first French counterattack on the Marne, supreme Allied commander, Marshal Foch unleashed his major offensive. It involved 435 tanks supported by aircraft and was preceded by only a brief artillery bombardment, giving it the element of surprise. The results were remarkable. French, British, and, most notably, Canadian troops pushed the enemy back as much as 10 miles (17 km). For the first time, German units were seen fleeing from the battlefield, and 6,000 prisoners were taken. Sensing that the tide had finally turned in the Allies' favor, Ludendorff called it the "Black Day of the German Army."

A renewed offensive on August 21 led to an organized German withdrawal to the Hindenburg Line. They had suffered heavy losses but so had the Allies and the fighting was far from over. Indeed, by early September the front lines were just about back to where they had been in January.

FORCING A CEASEFIRE

The August offensive had been what the Allies called "salient busting"— removing bulges in the line ready for a general advance. The next salient to be busted was that around St. Mihiel, taken by the French and Americans in mid-September. This left Foch free for a gigantic pincer movement, one arm

Allied advance: British infantry and tanks, with trench-crossing equipment, during the final phase of the war.

Feeling American power

"The . . . results of the victory . . . were very important. An American army was an accomplished fact, and the enemy had felt its power. No form of propaganda could overcome the depressing effect on the morale of the enemy of this demonstration of our ability to organize a large American force and drive it successfully through his defenses.
It gave our troops . . . confidence in their superiority and **raised their morale to the highest pitch.**"

From American General Pershing's report on the effects of the American victory at St. Mihiel. Quoted in www.firstworldwar.com/source/ stmihiel_pershing.htm attacking down the Meuse River toward Sedan, the other along the Lys River toward Antwerp. The southern front, largely featuring French and U.S. troops, set off on September 26. Meeting fierce resistance along the Kriemhilde Line but buoyed by American fresh-hearted confidence, the Allies pressed forward until they reached Sedan and Mézières in early November.

CEASEFIRE

The northern attack made similarly rapid progress. The Hindenburg Line was breached by October 5, and by November 9, the British were in Mons. Meanwhile, the Belgians captured all the coast and moved inland to Ghent. The Allies advanced on the Somme, too, taking St. Quentin and advancing toward Sedan. The situation in Germany was now so desperate that the high command was forced to call a ceasefire.

CROSS-REFERENCE AMERICAN UNITS ON THE WESTERN FRONT: PAGES 30–31 ARMISTICE: PAGES 42–43

Injured German prisoners of war carry a wounded colleague toward a U.S. dressing station in the Argonne, 1918.

Armistice Signed

At 11 a.m. on November 11, 1918, Germany and the Allies signed an armistice that brought all hostilities to a halt. Bulgaria, Turkey, and Austria-Hungary had already signed separate armistices. Actually, the Central Powers had proposed an armistice to U.S. President Wilson a month earlier but they could not accept his terms.

The new terms for Germany were extremely harsh. It had to evacuate all occupied territory, including Alsace and Lorraine, surrender its fleet and submarines, and cancel the Treaty of Brest-Litovsk. Details of the peace settlement were to be arranged at a conference in Versailles, near Paris, where the German Empire had been declared in 1871.

WORLDWIDE SUFFERING

The armistice marked the beginning of the end of the suffering for civilian populations as well. They had been massacred in Armenia, bombed in London, and millions had been driven from their homes in eastern France and western Russia. The collapse of the German, Austro-Hungarian, Russian, and Turkish Empires had led to widespread uncertainty and a general breakdown in law and order.

Life had been very hard even in countries that had not been invaded. By the end of 1916, 258 new laws had been passed in Germany limiting people's personal freedoms. The Allied blockade produced widespread starvation and a rise in diseases such as tuberculosis. In Britain, by the end of the war, 85 percent of food supply was regulated by the government. Even in the U.S., manufacture was controlled and personal freedoms limited by an Espionage Act. Finally, as the war ended, Europe was swept by a ghastly flu epidemic that killed more than the war itself.

VETERANS DAY

Lest they forget the misery and suffering, each town and village in Europe raised a plaque or memorial to those who had died. To this day, November 11—America's "Veterans Day"—is the day of remembrance for the terrible, unforgettable folly of the years 1914–18.

What now? German soldiers on their way home after the armistice of November 1917.

Never to return

"All those with whom I had really been intimate were gone; not one remained to share with me the heights and depths of my memories. As the years went by and youth departed and remembrance grew dim, a deeper and ever deeper darkness would come over the young men who were once my contemporaries. . . . The War was over; a new age was beginning; **but the dead were dead and would never return.**"

Vera Brittain, whose fiancé and only brother were killed in the war, records her feelings of November 1918 in her autobiography *Testament of Youth* (Victor Gollancz, 1933).

Victory—and peace! Joyful Parisians crowd the streets of the capital, November 1918.

CROSS-REFERENCE
THE PEACE SETTLEMENT: PAGES 44–45

Paris Peace Conference Opens

On January 12, 1919, the leaders of the victorious nations—Prime Ministers Clemenceau (France), Lloyd George (Britain), and Orlando (Italy), and President Wilson of the U.S.—sat down in Paris to sort out the dreadful chaos created by World War I.

Wilson had already set out his position in "Fourteen Points," seeking an international organization to settle disputes between countries and asking that peoples be free to choose their own governments. Clemenceau's position was more straightforward: punish Germany and ensure it would never again be able to wage war. Lloyd George tried to hold the line between the two, while Orlando wanted all he could get for Italy. Not surprisingly, the resulting treaties pleased no one.

GERMANY'S ALLIES

In September 1919, Austria accepted the Treaty of St. Germain by which its size was greatly reduced at the expense of Italy, Romania, and the new states of Yugoslavia and Czechoslovakia, and its population reduced from 30 million to 8 million. It was forbidden to unite with Germany, had to pay reparations to the victors, and was allowed only limited armed forces.

The Treaty of Neuilly (1919) imposed similarly harsh terms on Bulgaria, as did the Treaty of Trianon (1920) on

The victors in Paris (left to right): Prime Ministers Lloyd George and Orlando, Premier Clemenceau, and President Wilson.

Rejection of Versailles

Supreme Allied commander, Marshal Foch, condemned Versailles as too soft on Germany:
"This is not peace. It is an armistice for 20 years."

Quoted in www.channel4.com/history/microsites/F/firstworldwar/contwar_2.html

Meanwhile, Senator William E. Borah supported the Senate's rejection of Versailles because it proposed a League of Nations:
"It [the League] imperils what I conceive to be the underlying principles of this Republic. It is in conflict with the right of our people to govern themselves free from all restraint, legal or moral, of foreign powers."

Quoted in www.uschs.org/04_history/subs_timeline/04a_06.html

Hungary. Turkey was less easily dealt with. The first treaty, Sèvres (1920), was never ratified and, after a war with Greece, Turkey won more favorable terms at Lausanne (1923). This confirmed a modern Turkish state in place of the old Ottoman Empire.

VERSAILLES

The centerpiece of the conference was the Treaty of Versailles with Germany. By its humiliating terms, the losers had to accept responsibility for the war, pay a crippling 226 billion gold marks as reparations, and hand over territory to France, Belgium, Lithuania, Denmark, Czechoslovakia, and Poland. Many of the inhabitants of the surrendered areas were German-speaking.

Germany's future military capacity was to be severely limited and the Rhineland demilitarized. To ensure payment of the reparations, Allied forces occupied the heavily industrialized Ruhr Valley. With this, Germany's humiliation was complete. Criticism of Versailles was a major plank in the platform of the Nazi Party, which took power in 1933.

Five years on: exactly five years after the assassination at Sarajevo (see page 6), the Treaty of Versailles formally brings World War I to an end.

Key Figures in World War I

ALEXSEI BRUSILOV (1853–1926), RUSSIAN GENERAL

Alexsei Brusilov possessed unusual flair and imagination. He played a central part in Russia's advance into Galicia in 1914, and his 1916 summer offensive in the southwest greatly helped his allies on the Western Front. After serving the Provisional Government and heading the ill-fated Kerensky Offensive, he joined the communist Red Army.

GEORGES CLEMENCEAU (1841–1929), FRENCH PRIME MINISTER

At the age of 76, the tough Clemenceau ("the Tiger") became prime minister when France was at its lowest point in 1917. His rhetoric and determination boosted the nation's morale, leading to victory the following year. He had always been an admirer of the U.S. and was keen for it to fight alongside France.

DOUGLAS HAIG (1861–1928), BRITISH FIELD MARSHAL

Douglas Haig's reputation has see-sawed over the years. Immediately after the war he was a seen as a hero for his steely determination. He was then criticized as the "butcher" who had sacrificed men needlessly during the Somme, Arras, and Passchendaele offensives. Modern historians take a more balanced view, saying that by the standards of the day his soldiering was at least satisfactory.

PAUL VON HINDENBURG (1847–1934), GERMAN ARMY COMMANDER

In 1914, aristocratic Hindenburg was recalled from retirement and sent to confront the Russian attack on Prussia. His victories at Tannenberg and the Masurian Lakes gave him heroic status and in 1916 he was put in overall command of Central Power strategy. His defensive approach meant Germany was never invaded. Elected president of Germany in 1925, he appointed Adolf Hitler chancellor eight years later.

FRANZ CONRAD VON HÖTZENDORF (1852–1925), AUSTRIAN GENERAL

As commander of the large Austrian Army, Hötzendorf was eager for war with Serbia and Italy. However, he found warfare more testing than he had expected, especially against Serbia. His plans for a crushing blow against Italy in 1916 were cut short by the Brusilov Offensive. He was dismissed the following year.

MUSTAFA KEMAL (1881–1938), TURKISH SOLDIER AND POLITICIAN

The man who later became known affectionately as the "father of the Turks" made a name for himself when resisting the Allied landings in Gallipoli, 1915. He then led his units with skill in the Caucasus, where he was the only undefeated Turkish commander. After the war, he became the new Turkish Republic's first president and carried out a sweeping program of modernization.

DAVID LLOYD GEORGE (1863–1945), BRITISH PRIME MINISTER

Initially against the war, the intelligent and dynamic Lloyd George changed his mind after the German invasion of Belgium. Having made his mark as Minister of Munitions, he was appointed prime minister in December 1916. His skilled leadership guided the country to eventual victory. Of humble origins himself, he was not readily tolerant of those promoted because of family background, especially soldiers.

ERICH LUDENDORFF (1865–1937), GERMAN GENERAL

Ludendorff, an extremely able military planner, helped arrange the German offensive in 1914 and masterminded his country's victories over Russia on the Eastern Front. He worked very closely with the elderly Hindenburg and by 1918 the two wielded enormous power in Germany. However, after the failure of his Spring Offensives, his reputation suffered and in late 1918 he fled to Sweden in disguise at the end of the year.

NICHOLAS II (1896–1918), TSAR OF RUSSIA

Of no more than average intelligence, Nicholas was devoted to his family but lacked the qualities needed to rule an empire, especially in wartime. His decision to take personal control of strategy and his failure to ensure adequate supply to the troops at the front were catastrophic. Abandoned by everyone of real influence, he was forced to abdicate in 1917. He and his family were murdered the following year.

JOHN J. PERSHING (1860–1948), U.S. GENERAL

With the U.S.'s entry into the war in spring 1917, John Pershing had the unenviable task of building a huge U.S. army in double-quick time. He managed remarkably well. Despite inevitable setbacks, his AEF performed with great bravery and much skill. Unfortunately, he did not work with the other Allies as well as might have been expected and his relations with Foch, the supreme Allied commander, were always strained.

PHILIPPE PÉTAIN (1856–1951), FRENCH MARSHAL

Before the outbreak of war, Pétain warned about the difficulties of attack in modern conflict. His advice was ignored until he commanded the defense of Verdun in early 1916. His resistance made him a national hero and in May 1917 he was made commander-in-chief of the French Army. He ended his life in prison for treacherous cooperation with the Nazis in World War II.

WOODROW WILSON (1856–1924), U.S. PRESIDENT

Although attracted to the Allies, Wilson was reluctant to take his country into world war. Even when the U.S. was committed, he strove to bring about a wise and lasting peace. His idealistic "Fourteen Points" formed the basis of the post-war peace settlements but the Senate rejected his great dream—a League of Nations with the U.S. as a key player.

Glossary

AEF American Expeditionary Force

airship large, gas-filled balloon with engines and a cabin for the crew slung beneath

Allies France, Britain, Russia, the U.S., and other supporting nations

Anzac Australia and New Zealand Army Corps

armistice truce, formal ceasefire

Bolshevik Russian Communist group led by Lenin; the name means "majority"

Central Powers German, Austria-Hungary, Turkey, and other supporting nations

chancellor the head of the government in Germany; similar to a president or prime minister

convoy a number of ships traveling together for their own protection

deadlock when neither side in a conflict can make progress against the other

empire many states and peoples united under one controlling power. For example, in the nineteenth century, India, Canada, South Africa, and many other countries were in the British Empire.

entente agreement, less formal than a treaty

Gallipoli rocky peninsula to the west of the Dardanelles, the seaway leading from the Mediterranean to the Black Sea

Mesopotamia present-day Iraq

mobilize call up and prepare an army for war

mortar gun that fires a bomb on a high trajectory so that it falls directly onto a target

nationalist one who is passionately devoted to his or her country

offensive series of planned attacks over a wide area

reparations payments made as compensation for wrongs done

salient vulnerable bulge in a defensive line

scuttle deliberately sink one's own ship

sherif Muslim religious and secular ruler

soviet Communist committee

strategy overall war plans

Transjordan original name for Jordan

tsar hereditary ruler of Russia, from the word "Caesar"

U-boat German submarine

unification uniting several states and territories to make one big country

Further Information

BOOKS

Brendon, Vyvyen. *The First World War, 1914–18*. Hodder & Stoughton Educational, 2000.

Cawood, Ian. *The First World War*. Routledge, 2000.

Evans, David. *Teach Yourself the First World War*. Hodder, 2004.

Grant, Reg. *Armistice, 1918*. Hodder Wayland, 2000.

Hansen, Ole Steen. *The War in the Trenches*. Hodder Wayland, 2000.

Robson, Stuart. *The First World War*. Longman, 1998.

Ross, Stewart. *Atlas of Conflicts: World War I*. Watts, 2004.

Ross, Stewart. *Causes of the First World War*. Hodder Wayland, 2002.

Ross, Stewart. *Leaders of the First World War*. Hodder Wayland, 2002.

Ross, Stewart. *Technology of the First World War*. Hodder Wayland, 2003.

Ross, Stewart. *Battle of the Somme*. Hodder Wayland, 2003.

Wrenn, Andrew. *The First World War*. CUP, 1997.

FIRST-HAND ACCOUNTS

Britten, Vera. *Testament of Youth*. Victor Gollancz, 1933.

Graves, Robert. *Goodbye to All That*. Cassell, 1929.

Remarque, Erich Maria. *All Quiet on the Western Front*. Putnam, 1929.

Sassoon, Siegfried. *Memoirs of an Infantry Officer*. Faber, 1930.

Silkin, Jon, ed. *The Penguin Book of First World War Poetry*. Penguin, 1979.

WEBSITES

www.bbc.co.uk/history/worldwars/wwone
Excellent general information

www.pvhs.chico.k12.ca.us/~bsilva/projects/great_war/causes.htm
Useful summary of the causes of the war

www.channel4.com/history/microsites/F/firstworldwar/cont_war_2.html
Explores the war's controversies, especially how peace was made

www.spartacus.schoolnet.co.uk/FWWpolitical.htm
Full of useful material

PLACES TO VISIT

Imperial War Museum, London

Army Museum, London

Battlefields, graveyards, and war memorials of France, perhaps starting at Peronne and Albert.

Index